DISCOVERING PAINTINGS

SAINTS

Ruth Thomson

Chrysalis Children's Books

in association with The National Gallery, London

First published in the UK in 2003 by

Chrysalis Children's Books
An imprint of Chrysalis Books Group Plc
The Chrysalis Building
Bramley Road
London W10 6SP

Paperback edition first published in 2005

ISBN 1 84138 956 0 (hb)
ISBN 1 84458 460 7 (pb)

British Library in Publication data for this book is available from the British Library

Editorial manager: Joyce Bentley
Consultant: Erika Langmuir
Educational consultant: Hector Doyle
Design: Mei Lim
Illustrator: Georgie Birkett
Project manager for National Gallery Company: Jan Green

Printed in China

Contents

About this book

The pictures in this book show a variety of different saints. Some of the pictures depict important events in a saint's life. Saints are people honoured by the Christian Church after their death for being especially close to God. People were made saints for different reasons. Eleven of Jesus' followers are saints. They spread the message of Christ by preaching or writing books.

Many martyr saints lived in Roman times when most people worshipped many different gods. They were killed for worshipping only Christ and for refusing to give up their Christian beliefs. In paintings, martyr saints are often shown carrying palm leaves, a sign of victory over death.

Some saints started monasteries or friaries, places where people could come and devote their lives to God. They were known as founding saints.

Christian people often adopted the names of saints, dedicated cities in their honour and prayed to them for help. Some saints were thought to give people special protection in times of trouble or from particular diseases.

In paintings, saints often have golden discs, called haloes, around their heads as a sign of their holiness.

Saints and their attributes

Since most saints lived a long time before their pictures were
painted, artists did not know what they looked
like. Instead, artists usually painted saints
with features or clothes linked to their
lives, or with objects showing how they
were martyred (killed for their beliefs).
These are known as their attributes.
For instance, Saint Peter Martyr, who was murdered
in a wood in 1252, is shown with the weapons that
killed him. Saint Dominic, who founded a religious order,
is shown wearing a Dominican friar's white robe and black
cloak. Hundreds of years ago, people who could not read or write
could recognise the saints in pictures by these attributes.

Using this book

This book focuses on six main paintings of saints. There are four sections about
each painting that will help you to find out more about it.

 asks questions about the painting, which can
all be answered by looking at certain details.

 suggests activities that involve your senses
and your imagination.

 gives background information about the painting and
includes answers to some of the *Look Closer* questions.

 provides another painting on a similar theme for you
to compare and contrast with the first one.

The Coronation of the Virgin with Adoring Saints

(1370 – 1)

Attributed to Jacopo di Cione and Workshop

T his huge picture includes 48 different saints.
At the time the picture was made, most people
would have recognised them all.

LOOK CLOSER

Who do you think are the most important people in the picture?
How do you know? Do you know who they are?
Where do you think the scene is set?

Angels and saints surround the throne.
How can you tell which are which?

The artist has included objects to show which saint was which.
What objects can you see?

Find the Three Kings, who visited Jesus when he was born.
(Clue: they are all wearing identical crowns.)

How many martyr saints can you find?
(Clue: look for saints carrying palm leaves.)

TAKE ACTION

Can you spot the following saints?

- **Saint John the Baptist** – he told people about the coming of Christ. He lived in the desert and wore a camel skin.
- **Saint Peter** – he wears blue and yellow and holds the key to the gates of Heaven.
- **Saint John the Evangelist** – he has a long grey beard and holds the book he wrote – the Fourth Gospel of the New Testament.
- **Saint Stephen** – he was stoned to death, so he is shown with a stone on his head.

- **Saint Paul** – he wrote letters that became part of the New Testament. He was beheaded with a sword.
- **Saint Bartholomew** – he was skinned alive with a knife.
- **Saint Catherine** – she was tortured between spiked wheels.
- **Saint Lawrence** – he was roasted on a grill.
- **Saint Jerome** – he wears a red cardinal's hat.
- **Saint Dominic** – he wears a white tunic and black cloak and holds a white lily.
- **Saint Francis** – he wears a brown tunic.

The Court of Heaven

The three panels of the painting on page 6 were part of a huge altarpiece, made for a church in Italy. Although the church has been destroyed, we know what it looked like, because Saint Peter is holding a model of it.

The scene is set in Heaven. The artist imagined Heaven as if it were a king's court. Jesus sits on a throne crowning his mother, Mary, as Queen.

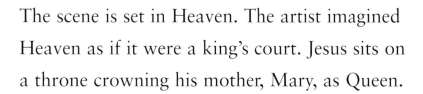

Winged angels play musical instruments at their feet and they are surrounded by saintly courtiers. These include some of Jesus' followers, such as Saint Matthew, who wrote one of the books of the New Testament, Saint Benedict, who founded a monastery, and his sister, Saint Scholastica, who founded a nunnery.

The saints did not live at the same time or in the same place, but the artist imagined that they all met in Heaven after they died. In the gloom of a church, lit only by candles, the golden haloes and embroidered clothes and hangings would have glittered and sparkled.

from left to right: *Saint John the Baptist, Saint Peter, Saint Catherine of Alexandria, Saint Dominic* (1476) **Carlo Crivelli**

These saints also formed part of an altarpiece for a church in Italy. Notice the textured gold background.

Each saint stands in a narrow, painted alcove. Their poses seem cramped. Look, for example, at Saint John's right arm.

Compare these saints with the same ones in Jacopo di Cione's picture on page 6
What is the same?
What is different?

Compare the saints' gazes.
Where might Saint Catherine be looking?
Why might Saint Dominic be looking downwards?

9

The Wolf of Gubbio

(1437 – 44)
Sassetta

A ferocious wolf once terrorised the small Italian town of Gubbio, attacking anyone who went into the woods beyond the town gates.

Luckily, Saint Francis came to the rescue. He persuaded the wolf to stop eating people if, in return, the town agreed to feed it every single day.

LOOK CLOSER

What can you *see* on the ground behind the wolf?
How has the artist shown that the wolf
had *been* eating people over quite a long time?

How do Saint Francis and the wolf agree on their pact?
Why do you think Saint Francis has turned towards
the man with the pen and inkwell?

Why is Saint Francis meeting the wolf outside the town walls?
Why is everyone crowded behind Saint Francis?

Who *else* is watching Saint Francis?
Why are they up on the battlements?

TAKE ACTION

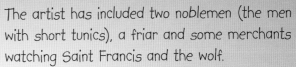

See if you can find:
- **three knots on Saint Francis' belt**
  (These represent his three vows of poverty,
  chastity and obedience.)
- **three women wearing head-bands**
- **three men wearing black hats**

If you were Saint Francis what would you
ask the man with the pen and ink to write?
What sort of food would you give to the wolf?

The artist has included two noblemen (the men
with short tunics), a friar and some merchants
watching Saint Francis and the wolf.
If this event happened today, what sort of
people would you include as the witnesses?

Imagine what the two noblemen might
be saying to one another.
- Do you think they are pleased with
  Saint Francis?
- Do you think they are afraid of the wolf?

The Life of Saint Francis

These four pictures show some other important incidents in Saint Francis' life. Francis was the son of a cloth merchant. One night, after giving his clothes to a poor knight, he dreamed about a castle. An angel explained that this meant Francis should start an army of friars to fight for the Church.

Saint Francis meets a knight poorer than himself, and *Saint Francis' vision of the Founding of the Franciscan order* (1437 – 44) **Sassetta**

When Francis sold some of his father's cloth to pay for a church to be restored, his father was so angry that he threatened to disown him. Francis threw off his fine clothes saying that, in future, he would only recognise God as his father. Francis then gathered 12 disciples and went to Rome. There, the Pope blessed them and granted Francis the right to preach.

Saint Francis renounces his Earthly Father (1437 – 44) **Sassetta**

The Stigmatisation of Saint Francis
(1437 – 44) **Sassetta**

One day, while praying in the mountains, Francis saw a vision of Christ on a fiery cross. From then on, his hands, feet and side bled from wounds that mysteriously appeared in the same places as the wounds Christ had received on the cross. These wounds are known as the *stigmata*.

Francis tried to convert a Moslem Sultan to Christianity. He offered to walk through fire with one of the Sultan's priests to prove his faith.

When Francis died, a bystander at the funeral wanted to touch his body to prove that Francis really had received the *stigmata*.

Saint Francis before the Sultan
(1437 – 44) **Sassetta**

Saint George and the Dragon

(ABOUT 1460)

Paolo Uccello

Saint George was a warrior saint. He is said to have saved a princess from a dreadful dragon, who was about to eat her. His story sounds like a fairy tale. Do you think this really happened? Do you think dragons really exist?

LOOK CLOSER

What is Saint George doing?

What has the princess done?
How would you describe her mood?

Who do you feel sorry for in this picture? Why?

Uccello has left out something particular
from his painting which makes the figures
and animals look very odd.
Can you work out what they are?
(Clue: You can only see these on sunny days.)

Does this picture feel noisy or quiet to you?
What makes you say that?

What time of day do you think it is?

TAKE ACTION

Stand in the same pose as the dragon.
Pretend your arms are wings.
How does it feel?

**What does the dragon's
pose tell you about how he feels?**

Stand in the same pose as the princess.
**Would you stand that way if you
were near a dragon?**

How might you stand instead?

Shapes in art can send messages.
**Can you find five rounded, curling shapes
and five spiky shapes in the picture?**

**What do you notice about where
these different shapes are?**

**How do they affect the mood and energy
of the picture?**

Make up your own story that fits the picture
better. Think why the dragon might look
so sad and the princess might be so calm.

The Story of Saint George

According to the Golden Legend, a book of medieval tales about saints, a loathsome dragon with foul, fiery breath once menaced a city near a lake. The local people tried to keep it away by giving it two sheep to eat each day. However, before long, there were hardly any sheep left and everyone was in danger of starving. The king decided to offer the dragon human victims instead.

These were drawn by lot and eventually the lot fell on the king's daughter. She was taken, like all the other victims, to the dragon's cave and left to be eaten. As she waited in despair, George rode past on his white horse.

He promised, in the name of Christ, to help her. When the dragon appeared, George fearlessly attacked it. The princess tied her belt around the neck of the defeated beast and led it back to the city, where George killed it.

Uccello has put two parts of the story together – George attacking the dragon and the princess with the dejected, subdued dragon tied on a lead, like a pet.

LOOK FURTHER

Saint George and the Dragon
(PROBABLY 1560 – 80) **Jacopo Tintoretto**

Tintoretto's picture of Saint George and the Dragon is far more action-packed than Uccello's. The weather is windier and stormier.

Notice how the billowing clothes of the princess and Saint George and the twisting neck of the dragon help to suggest movement.

What has Tintoretto included in the story that Uccello has not?

Which person has *been* made to look the most important?

Who do you think the person in the sky might be?

Does this version of the story look realistic to you?

What do you think has happened to the man lying on the ground?

The Martyrdom of Saint Sebastian

(COMPLETED 1475)

Antonio and Piero del Pollaiuolo

S aint Sebastian was a soldier in Ancient Rome. When the Roman Emperor, Diocletian, discovered that Sebastian had become a Christian, he cruelly ordered Sebastian's fellow soldiers to tie him to a tree and shoot him dead with arrows.

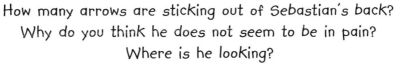

 LOOK CLOSER

How many arrows are sticking out of Sebastian's back?
Why do you think he does not seem to be in pain?
Where is he looking?

What similarities can you see in the archers' positions?
What shape have the artists used to arrange
Sebastian and the six archers?

How would you describe the soldiers' expressions?
How do you think they feel about shooting Sebastian?

Behind Sebastian, the artists have painted a distant view
of the landscape around Florence, where they lived.
What clue have they included to remind you
that Sebastian came from Ancient Rome?

Sebastian has been tied almost naked to a tree.
What other religious martyr does he remind you of?

TAKE ACTION

Can you spot these things?
- quivers full of arrows
- two silhouettes facing one another
  These are the profiles of Moors' heads,
  the emblem of the Pucci family who built
  the church where this picture used to hang.
- three horses leaping
- a man leading a horse

Imagine you can step inside the picture
and take a walk around.
Where will you start? Where will you go?
Describe what you pass and see if other people
can follow your route.

Pretend you are one of the soldiers who has to
report back to the Emperor. Based on the picture,
describe what you did and how Sebastian reacted.
What happened after the moment shown here?
Did Sebastian say anything to you? Did he die?

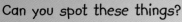

The Plague Saint

The picture on page 18 looks very gruesome, but Sebastian did not, in fact, die from his arrow wounds. Although the soldiers left him for dead on the tree, some holy women nursed him back to health.

When he recovered, Sebastian went to see the Emperor. He told him that he could serve both God and the Emperor at the same time. The Emperor did not believe him and ordered the soldiers to batter him to death with clubs.

At the time this picture was painted, there was a deadly disease raging, called the plague. Sebastian's arrow wounds reminded people of the boils which appear on the skin of victims of the plague. Since Sebastian did not die from his wounds, people believed that praying to the saint would protect them or cure them from the plague.

The picture was painted as an altarpiece for a church in Florence, which housed the saint's arm bones. The landscape looks like the Arno valley around Florence; but the broken triumphal arch resembles those in Rome, where Sebastian was killed.

The soldiers are using crossbows and longbows and the knights on horseback are wearing plate armour, none of which existed in Ancient Rome.

Saints Fabian and Sebastian
(ABOUT 1475 – 82) **Giovanni di Paolo**

Compare this picture of Saint Sebastian with the one on page 18. Here, Saint Sebastian stands beside Saint Fabian, a sainted pope.

These two saints share the same feast day – when people celebrate the life of a saint, with a special church service and, sometimes, with a procession.

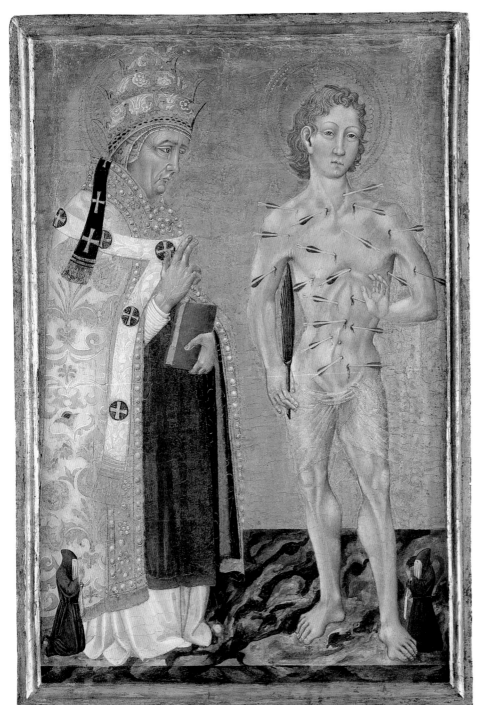

How many arrows are sticking out of Saint Sebastian?

Do you think he would have survived a shooting like this?

What effect do the two tiny kneeling figures have on the picture?

How has the artist made Saint Fabian seem an important person?

How has the artist made Saint Fabian look old and Saint Sebastian look young?

The Conversion of Saint Hubert

(ABOUT 1480)

Master of the Life of the Virgin

One Good Friday, Hubert, a rich nobleman, was out riding in the woods with his servant and his hunting dogs.

Out of the blue, he saw something unexpected caught between the branched antlers of a mighty stag.

Can you see what it was?

What do you think Hubert was doing in the woods?
What clues has the artist given you? Why is he kneeling now?

How can you tell that Hubert was a rich man?
How can you tell that he is also a saint?
What makes him stand out in the picture?

Do you think Hubert's servant knows what Hubert has seen?
How can you tell?

How many huntsmen can you see? How many hunting dogs are there?

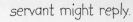

How has the artist shown that the stag is startled?

TAKE ACTION

Look closely at the picture and see if you can discover the following people, animals, things and places:
- a hunter with a spear and a dog
- a dog with a red studded collar
- a hunting horn
- two dogs sniffing in the woods
- a castle with two towers
- a stag being chased by dogs

Make up your own story of this picture so far . . . what do you think will happen next? Think what Hubert might tell his servant and what his servant might reply.
Where do they go? What do they do?

How has the artist used colour to distinguish between the foreground, the middle and background of the picture?
- Why did he put people in the background as well as the foreground?
- Where did he want to draw your attention first?

Saint Hubert's Vision

Hubert, a rich nobleman, went hunting on Good Friday, instead of going to church, as all good Christians did, to remember the time when Jesus Christ was crucified. While he was riding through the woods, Hubert saw a vision of the Crucifixion between the antlers of a stag.

He immediately fell on his knees and vowed to devote himself to God. The artist of the picture on page 22 has shown Hubert dressed in rich and fashionable clothes, but has also given him a halo to show that he later became a saint. Hubert stayed in the woods as a hermit, but then became a bishop and founded a church.

In this second painting by the same artist, called *The Mass of Saint Hubert*, Hubert is a bishop, standing at the altar of his church. He looks different because his hair has been cut, but there is a clue that this is the same person. Can you spot something in the foreground which is the same as in the hunting picture?

When Hubert died, he was buried under this church altar. A hundred years later, his body was taken out in the presence of a prince and a bishop, and found to be perfectly preserved. This was considered proof of his holiness.

 **LOOK FURTHER**

This picture shows another saint who had a similar vision to Saint Hubert's. It is set in a forest outside Rome.

The sight of a glowing crucifix between the antlers of a stag converted this Roman commander to Christianity.

What animals and birds live in the forest?

How does Saint Eustace react to what he has seen?

How does the artist show that the hunt is still on?

How has the artist made Saint Eustace stand out?

The Virgin and Child with Saints and Donor

(PROBABLY 1510)

Gerard David

This picture shows the imaginary walled garden of Paradise, where the Virgin Mary reigns as Queen. The artist has set it in a real place, the town where he lived. Three women saints keep Mary company.

LOOK CLOSER

The donor, who paid for the picture to be painted, is the man kneeling.
Why do you think the artist put him in the garden?
How can you tell he was rich? Why is he kneeling?

Do you think the saints knew one another?
How can you tell?
(Clue: look at their expressions.)

What season do you think it is? How do you know?

Saint Catherine's attribute is a wheel.
Where is it?
Saint Barbara's attribute is a tower.
Can you find two towers in the picture?

The chapel where this picture hung was named
after another saint, called Anthony Abbot.
Where can you see him in the picture?

TAKE ACTION

Can you spot these things?
• an angel picking grapes
• a string of red beads
• the donor's prayer book
• a red rose

Gerard David painted in oils. He contrasted
warm colours, such as red, orange and yellow,
with cool colours, such as green, blue and violet,
to give a rich and interesting effect. Find three
places in the picture where a warm colour and
a cool one have been put side by side.

Which of these shapes can you see?

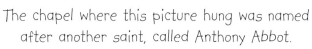

Which of these forms can you see?

• How do the shapes affect the atmosphere
of the picture?
• Does it feel still or full of movement?

27

Three Women Saints

The donor ordered the picture shown on page 26 for the chapel where his mother was buried. To honour her memory, he asked the artist to paint three female saints. The artist has painted their meeting in the Virgin's garden where flowers are always in bloom. No-one looks at anyone else and all sit perfectly still. The Virgin Mary, Christ's mother, sits in the centre, to show her importance.

Catherine, a princess of the Ancient Roman empire, became a Christian. The emperor wanted to marry her, but she refused, saying she was 'the bride of Christ'. (Here, she is shown receiving a wedding ring from the Christ Child.) The furious emperor ordered her to be torn apart between spiked wheels. According to legend, a bolt of lightning shattered the wheels without Catherine being harmed. The emperor ordered her to be beheaded by the sword instead. The wheel and the sword became her attributes.

Barbara was said to be so beautiful that her father locked her in a tower to prevent men chasing after her. When she then became a Christian, her cruel father told the authorities. They ordered him to kill her. After Barbara's death, her father was struck by lightning and burnt to ashes.

Mary Magdalene followed Christ and washed his feet with perfume. Her attribute is a lidded jar.

The Virgin and Child with Saints and Donors
(PROBABLY ABOUT 1475) **Hans Memling**

Can you find five similarities between this picture and David's painting? How do the backgrounds differ?

Notice how the two women saints are presenting the donors to the Virgin Mary with their outstretched hands.

Who are the donors of this picture?

Find Saint Catherine's sword and wheel. (Clue: the wheel is part of a building.)

What are the angels doing?

Why might the artist have included two towers as Barbara's attributes?

Things to do

Each one of these six activities is related to one of the pictures in this book. Before you start, look back at the painting to help you remember all about it.

The Coronation of the Virgin with Adoring Saints

The objects that saints hold tell people something about their lives. Draw a picture of yourself with an object that would tell people something about you and your interests.

The Wolf of Gubbio

Imagine you are the wolf that met Saint Francis. Write or draw a list of the foods that you would like the people in the town to give you. It can be as delicious or disgusting as you like.

Saint George and the Dragon

Draw your own scary dragon for Saint George to fight. Give it the head of one animal, the body and tail of another, the feet and claws of another and the wings of a bat or a bird.

The Martyrdom of Saint Sebastian

Draw your own version of Saint Sebastian and the six archers. Give everyone a thought *bubble*. Write in the *bubbles* what each person might *be* thinking.

The Conversion of Saint Hubert

Saint Hubert had *several* hunting dogs. Draw the one you would most like to own. Include a sturdy, studded collar with your name on it.

The Virgin and Child with Saints and Donor

Are these statements about the picture of the Virgin and Child on page 26 true or false?

1. The Virgin is looking at Saint Catherine.

2. The donor is praying with his eyes open.

3. A strong wind is blowing in the garden.

4. The dog is wearing a red collar.

5. Saint Barbara is holding a small metal box.

6. Mary Magdalene is wearing a veil.

Glossary

altarpiece
A painting or sculpture, set on or above a Christian altar to help focus worship during church services.

donor
A person who orders a picture from an artist, usually featuring themself, and then gives it to a church.

emblem
Anything used like a badge to identify a person, family or organisation.

halo
A disc or circle of light, usually painted in gold, surrounding the head of holy persons, such as Jesus, the Virgin Mary, saints and angels.

hermit
Someone living alone, often in a remote place, who has no contact with other people.

martyr
Someone who suffers or is put to death for his or her beliefs.

merchant
A person who makes a living by buying and selling goods.

paradise
Another word for heaven – believed by Christians to be the home of God, saints and angels.

silhouette
The outline shape of a person or thing usually filled in black.

Index